Leaving Well Activity Book is accompanied by a number of printable online materials, designed to ensure this resource best supports your needs.

The **Coping Cube** and **Awards Ceremony** pages are available online to be downloaded and printed for easy use.

Go to https://resourcecentre.routledge.com/speechmark and click on the cover of this book.

Answer the question prompt using your copy of the book to gain access to the online content.

"The *Moving On* series gives all who work with children a powerful, practical tool to help them 'leave well so they can enter well'. As each book focuses on a particular stage of the moving process, children can find words and create images to express the often-paradoxical feelings any move can make. I highly recommend it!"

Ruth E. Van Reken, co-author of *Third Culture Kids: Growing Up Among Worlds*

Leaving Well Activity Book

Moving from country to country is no small feat. This activity book is designed for use with children aged 6–12 to help those on the move to navigate the process of global transition smoothly. Based on the latest relocation and transition research, wellbeing boosting strategies are shared for transition and beyond.

Children are introduced to mindful activities and are encouraged to use their creativity by annotating and illustrating the pages as they move through the book, allowing them to be an active participant in their move. *Leaving Well Activity Book* helps children to reflect on how they feel about the move, to remember other moves and understand that change is a part of life. Full of valuable strategies to boost wellbeing as they move forward, the text highlights top tips for expressing feelings that will help children prepare for departure. The book normalises mixed feelings, helping the child acknowledge their hopes and fears and reflect on their sense of control. This book can be used effectively alongside:

Arriving Well Activity Book which helps the child settle in their new place, to reflect on the move and understand that change is a part of life.

Moving On Facilitator's Guide which offers guidance notes and prompts to help bring out the best experience for the child and is designed to help the adult feel confident in their delivery and in responding to any questions. It contains key points to consider, examples of 'what you could say', as well as explains the theory behind the workbook activities.

Acting as a tool for engagement, *Leaving Well Activity Book* will help children come to terms with the move and help adults support children preparing to leave for a new country.

Claire Holmes is Head of School Counselling at Tanglin Trust School, Singapore where she leads a team of counsellors who work across the whole school K-13. Claire's counselling modality is strength-based, empowering others to access their own inner wisdom and knowing. Her practice incorporates expressive therapies, mindfulness, and solution-focused interventions. In her role, she teaches mindfulness-based stress reduction (MBSR) to parents and staff.

Leaving Well Activity Book

Leaving Well Activity Book is part of a set – Moving On: Activity Books and Guide to Support Children Relocating to a New Country.

Book 1 – *Leaving Well Activity Book: Therapeutic Activities to Support Kids Aged 6-12 who are Moving to a New Country.*

Book 2 – *Arriving Well Activity Book: Therapeutic Activities to Support Kids Aged 6-12 who have Moved to a New Country.*

Book 3 – *Moving On Facilitator's Guide: How to Support Children Relocating to a New Country.*

Leaving Well Activity Book

Therapeutic Activities to Support Kids Aged 6-12 who are Moving to a New Country

Claire Holmes

Routledge
Taylor & Francis Group

LONDON AND NEW YORK

Designed cover image: Claire Holmes

First published 2024
by Routledge
4 Park Square, Milton Park, Abingdon, Oxon OX14 4RN

and by Routledge
605 Third Avenue, New York, NY 10158

Routledge is an imprint of the Taylor & Francis Group, an informa business

British Library Cataloguing-in-Publication Data
A catalogue record for this book is available from the British Library

ISBN: 978-1-032-46683-5 (pbk)
ISBN: 978-1-003-38283-6 (ebk)

DOI: 10.4324/9781003382836

Typeset in Tekton Pro
by KnowledgeWorks Global Ltd.

Printed in the UK by Severn, Gloucester on responsibly sourced paper

Access the Support Material: https://resourcecentre.routledge.com/speechmark

Dedication:

Dedicated to my companions on my global adventuring: My husband, Chris, my two Third Culture Kids, Hana and Ben, Neo the Scottie Dog, and Milo the tabby cat.

Acknowledgement:

These books would not have been possible without my International School journey, thank you Chris Holmes for initiating our overseas experience and what a blast it's been. Special acknowledgment goes to Hana Holmes for helping me reflect on content and layout; your creativity astounds me. Heartfelt thanks to my Tanglin Trust School Counselling Colleagues, past and present; Kendra Frazier, Valerie Hoglan, Paula Huggins, Pippa Gresham, Simon Parkin, Seunghee Chung, Jo Bush, Kevin Dunk, and Tash McCarroll; you have been unflagging sources of wisdom, inspiration, and compassion. Lastly, deep appreciation goes to my wonderfully wise School Counselling Supervisor, Helen Wilson, thank you for being my guru.

Welcome!

You've been given this book because you are moving to a new country. Each page has a different activity. You'll get creative by drawing; colouring, writing, and making things.

It's a book that helps you learn about leaving well. If you leave well, most likely, you'll arrive well too. Using this book will help you have a good last few weeks and make a great start in your new place.

My name is _____

I am moving from _____ to
_____

Where are you now?

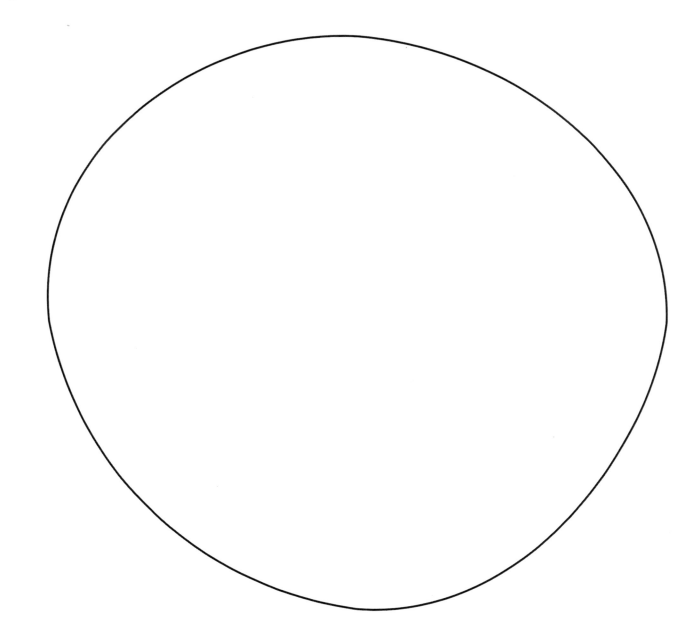

2 Draw something in the circle above to represent the country you live in now.

Change happens.

Change is a normal part of life, we've all been through transitions (which means moving from one thing to another). Perhaps you have moved from one school to another or from country to country. You might have moved from one sports team to another or moved house, these are transitions too.

Fill in the gaps... I remember moving from:

_____ to _____

Draw something above to go with your move.
Write something below that helped with the move:

Moving on graph.

Here is a graph showing how you might feel when you move from one place to another. The thin, jagged black line that runs through the middle represents your wellbeing.

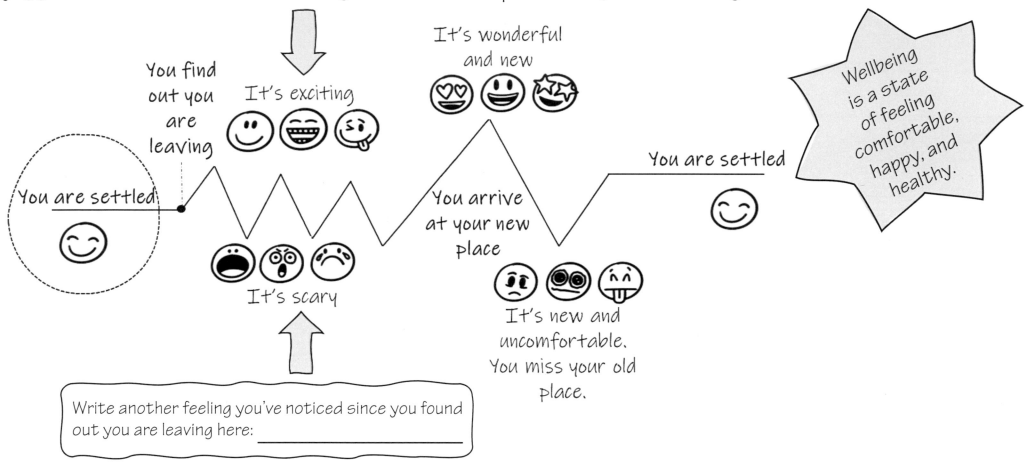

The circle represents you before you knew you were moving. Most likely, you were happy and okay most of the time. Then you heard you were leaving, this moved you along to the small black dot. Now, you find yourself at the grey arrows. You might be feeling excited and scared and a variety of other emotions too.

Moving on takes GUTS².

Moving country needs bravery. Some people use the expression 'it takes guts' to describe being brave. Each letter of the word **G-U-T-S²** stands for something that will help leave well. Paying attention to each of these will make your transition as smooth as possible.

Wondering what the ² is for? It's there because we have an extra S, which needs attention to leave well.

G oodbye
(Say goodbye)

U nload feelings
(Share how you feel)

T hank you
(Let people know you appreciate them)

S elf-care
(Look after yourself)

S ay hello
(Get curious about your new country)

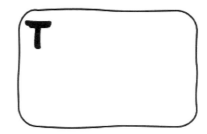

Draw something in each of the five blocks on the left to represent what each letter stands for.

People power.

G G is for? _____

Write the names of people you want to say goodbye to on these body outlines:

Add more people if you need to. There may be different groups of people who you know from different places.

Doing something with a group of people or an individual helps leave well. Let's get planning:

Where?

What?

When?

Who?

- -

Where?

What?

When?

Who?

Show your parent/s or guardians your plan/s to see what's possible. Talk about what needs to be done. Sometimes plans need a bit of adjustment!

Remember: Goodbyes may **not be forever**; they **may not be the end**; they simply mean farewell until you meet again.

Leaving things behind.

Moving to another country might mean your animals can't come with you. Make sure you find a way to say goodbye and remember them. You may be able to visit their new home and help settle them in.

There may be special items that are too fragile, large, or unsuitable to take; get creative with saying goodbye to these too.

Shoot as many goodbye photos as you can to take with you!

Where are your special places? They might include a restaurant, park, or a favourite spot where you enjoy a hobby? Write or draw your favourite places to visit before you leave below:

Tick them off when you've visited!

Lighten the load.

Goodbyes

There may be people who you used to be friends with but now are not. You might still feel upset with this person or they you. Saying goodbye to those who have upset you, and saying sorry if you need to, helps you forgive; let go of bad feelings and feel lighter.

Write the names, or draw a symbol, of anyone below you'd like to forgive or someone who might need to forgive you:

'Clearing the air' means getting rid of bad feelings, usually by talking.

Talk to an understanding adult about ways to say goodbye.

Remember: You may meet up again at some point, 'clearing the air' now will make it easier if you do.

Feelings faces.

U is for?

_____

Everyone has lots of feelings at times of change, all are okay. Write a feeling on each of the lines and draw a matching emoji to go with it in the circle above.

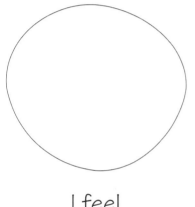

I feel

_____

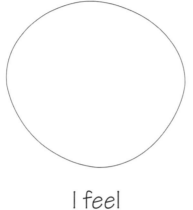

I feel

_____

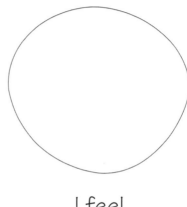

I feel

_____

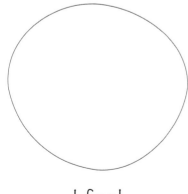

I feel

_____

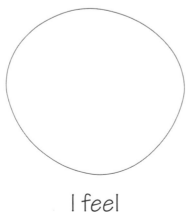

I feel

_____

I feel

_____

Draw feelings out.

Bring to mind a feeling (look at page 9 if you need to).
Write the feeling here: _____

Answer the questions below and draw your feeling in the box.

Unload feelings

Where do you feel it in your body? _____

Does your feeling have a colour? _____

Does it have a shape? _____

How big or small is it? _____

Is it moving or still? _____

Does it have a temperature? _____

Does it have a texture, smell, and/or taste?

_____

A sound? _____

Is there anything else to say about your feeling?

_____

Draw your feeling here:

Talk feelings out.

Talking to someone about how you feel will help you leave well.
Draw or write below who you can talk to over the next few weeks.

 MY HELPERS

Remember: A problem shared is a problem halved.

Unload feelings

And there's more.

Here are other ways to unload feelings.
Colour in the boxes below which contain things that might help you.
Feel free to add more of your own.

Tell an animal or cuddly toy about how you feel.

Write a feelings poem.

Write your feelings in a diary or journal.

Speak out loud how you feel to yourself.

Sculpt a feeling with clay.

Write some song lyrics about how you feel.

Draw or paint how you feel using colours, shapes, and lines.

Write a message to a trusted person sharing how you feel.

Play a musical instrument in a way that shows your feelings.

Move your body in a way that shows how you feel.

Hopes and fears flower.

At times of change, it's normal to have lots of different hopes and fears, these are feelings too.

Unload feelings

Write or draw your fears about your move in the petals and your hopes in the centre of the flower. Some will be the same as others who are moving and some will be unique to you.

Unique means special to you.

Who and how?

T is for? _____

Saying thank you makes others and you feel great. **WHO** are the people who have made a difference in your time here? **HOW** will you say thank you?

There are many ways you can do this: talk to them, give them a card, a gift, or send them an electronic message. You may have some other ideas – get creative! Fill in the grid below.

WHO?

HOW?

Remember: Just because you are moving doesn't mean your current friendships and relationships will end. Saying thank you may help them last longer.

Thank you

Staying connected.

Most likely, some people you thank, you'll want to stay in touch with. Think about who those people are, how you would do this, and how often you hope to be in contact with them. Fill in the grid below:

Who?	How will you do this? Add contact details in this column if you like.	How often?

What brings me joy?

S S is for? _____

Self-care is about looking after you. When you pay attention to yourself in a kind way, you are able to cope with change, feel positive, and make good choices.

What brings me joy?
Draw or write down activities that bring you joy below:

Make time to do some of these even though moving is busy.

MY WELLBEING BOOST

Self-care

What does my body tell me?

Times of change might make you feel out of control, worried, or upset. You might say you feel stressed.

Even though I feel stressed, I know I've got GUTS[2]!

Listen to your body, it will tell you when it's time to choose a way of coping. Turn to page 18 to find out more...

Draw on this body outline where you feel 'stress' in your body. Use colours, shapes, and/or lines.

17

Self-care

How *do* I *cope* well?

Colour in the squares below which contain things that might help steady yourself when you feel stressed. Different people find different things helpful.

Take a few deep breaths.	Listen to music or play an instrument.	Get a drink of water and/or splash cold water on your face.	Play with a favourite pet or toy.	Imagine a beautiful and peaceful place.
Talk with a trusted adult or friend.	Move your body however you like, e.g. do some jumping jacks, play outside, or skip.	Say something calming to yourself like 'It's okay, I've got this'.	Write down or draw how you are feeling.	Do some art or make something.

Add one more of your own here: _____

Self-care

What encouraging things can I say to myself?

Write down some encouraging messages to say to yourself when you feel worried or upset in the speech bubbles.

Self-care

1. Write or draw things you CAN control inside the hand, examples might be 'my breathing' or 'how I speak to friends'.

2. Write or draw things you CAN'T control outside of the hand, examples might be 'how friends behave' or 'the weather'.

3. Add things that you CAN and CAN'T control about your move.

What's in and out of my control?

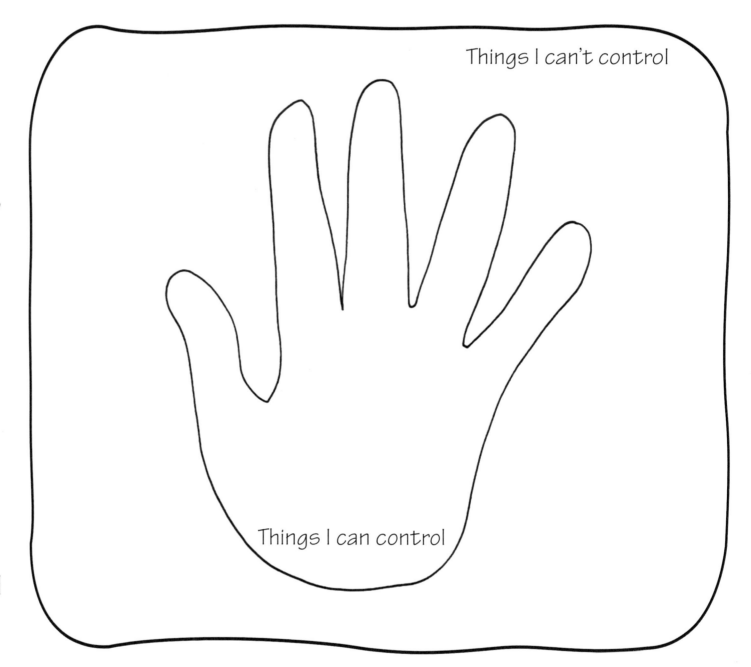

Things I can't control

Things I can control

Mindful colouring.

Grab some coloured pencils or pens and try mindful colouring. Take slow, deep breaths. Try playing soothing music. Doing something for you is important when things get busy.

Take 5.

Breathing well helps you cope when big emotions arrive. Try this Take 5 technique to steady yourself:

Technique means a special way of doing something that you can practise.

1. Stretch your hand out like a star.
2. Get your index finger ready on the other hand (that's the one you point with).
3. Begin by placing your index finger at the bottom on the outside of your thumb.
4. Take a big breath in and as you do this, move your index finger up the outside of the thumb.
5. Pause at the top of your thumb.
6. As you breathe out, trace down the inside of your thumb.
7. Pause at the bottom.
8. Repeat on the next finger and then continue with the whole hand.
9. Repeat as you need to.

Practise Take 5 when you feel okay.

When you get used to it, try it when your body lets you know you feel 'stressed' (look at page 17 to remind yourself how your body does this).

22

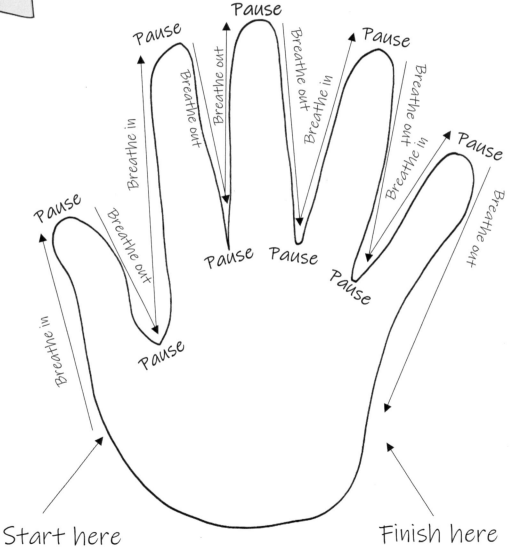

Start here

Finish here

Thankfulness tree.

Paying attention to things you feel thankful for lifts your mood.

Write or draw 10 things you are thankful for in each of the thankfulness tree leaves on the right.

TRY THIS:

1. Read one of your leaves out loud; 'I am thankful for… (say what's on your leaf)'.
2. Close your eyes and imagine whatever is on that leaf.
3. Take a big breath in through your nose and breathe out through your mouth.

REPEAT FOR THE REST OF THE LEAVES.

Self-care

Stand like a tree.

Even in windy weather trees are strong, solid, and firmly rooted to the ground. When you need to feel strong and brave, practise standing like a tree:

1. Stand still, notice your feet firmly planted on the ground.
2. Stand tall, extend your neck and head upwards, lift your chin slightly.
3. Drop your shoulders back and down.
4. Imagine that a gentle breeze is making your body sway and your arms gently move; keep your feet firmly planted.
5. Imagine the wind getting stronger, make your body movements bigger; keep your feet rooted.
6. Imagine the weather has passed. Stand still, notice how that feels.
7. Take a few deep breaths and say to yourself 'I am like a tree, brave and strong whatever the weather'.

**Practise standing like a tree when you feel okay.
When you get used to it, try it when you need to feel brave and strong.**

Get curious.

S

Our second S is for?

S _____

Find a time to ask these questions when you all have time to consider them carefully.

Getting curious about your new place will help leave well.
Ask your parent/s or guardians some questions:

- What will my new school be like?
- Can I contact any new classmates to start to make friends?
- What will our new home be like? What will my bedroom be like?
- What will our new country be like? (Language/food/weather?)

If you have other questions you'd like to ask, write them in the box below:

Say hello

Curiouser and curiouser....

The more you know about where you're going, the better prepared you'll be.

Find some fun facts about your new country and write them above, you can draw things if you like too.

Say hello

Ballooning around.

Let's think about what you are looking forward to and things that might be challenging about your new place. Being realistic helps you arrive well.

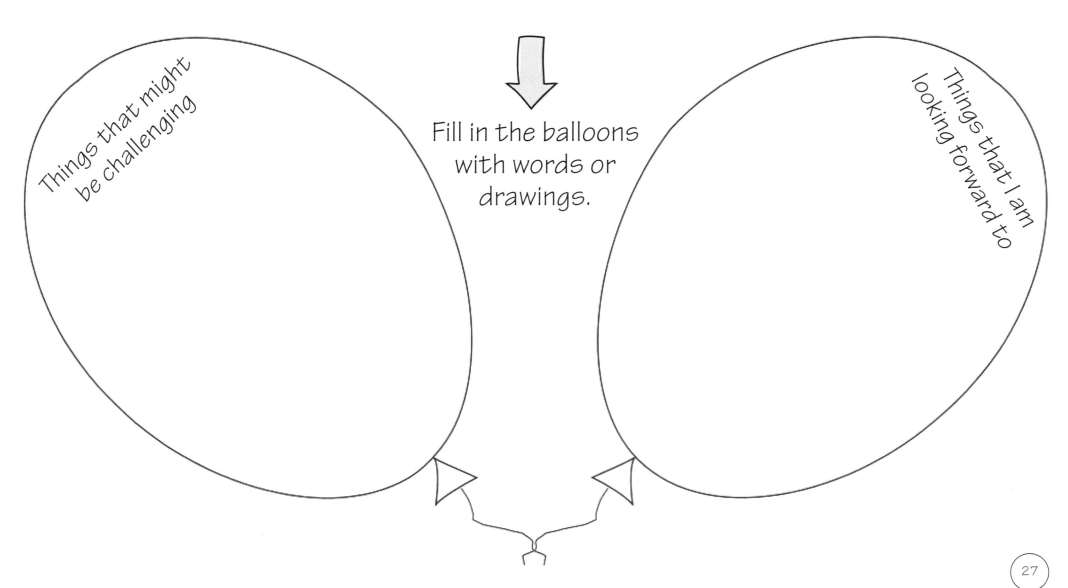

Things that might be challenging

Fill in the balloons with words or drawings.

Things that I am looking forward to

Gallery of strengths.

Strengths are positive character traits that you and others notice. Using your strengths helps you be the best version of yourself. Have a look at the examples below (you can probably think of many more).

Character traits are qualities that make you who you are.

Kind, caring, funny, patient, trusting, friendly, grateful, loyal, helpful, joyful, honest, determined, brave, creative, respectful, and peaceful.

Write six of your strengths on the lines on the right. Draw your strength in action in the frame above each line.

GET CREATIVE;
draw a funky frame around each picture.

Moving on poem.

My bags are packed, boxes have gone,
goodbyes feel hard, faces are long.
I hope we'll meet again one day,
it's time to go, I'm on my way.

2) Write your own four-line poem about moving here:

1) Use this brain-dump box to get all your ideas down:

Moving on podium.

Write down three things that you'd like to remember from this activity book in the boxes below.

Rank them 1–3, with 1 being the most helpful.

1

2

3

Coping Cube.

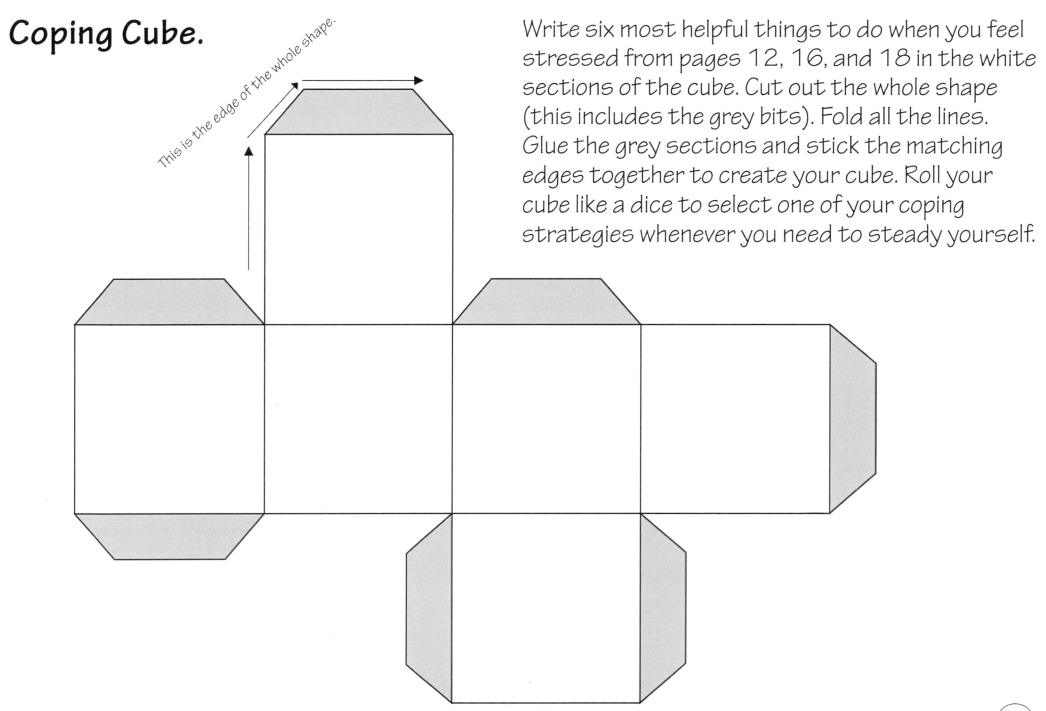

This is the edge of the whole shape.

Write six most helpful things to do when you feel stressed from pages 12, 16, and 18 in the white sections of the cube. Cut out the whole shape (this includes the grey bits). Fold all the lines. Glue the grey sections and stick the matching edges together to create your cube. Roll your cube like a dice to select one of your coping strategies whenever you need to steady yourself.

Awards Ceremony.

Read the stickers below. Choose a page that goes with each of them. Colour in the sticker, cut it out, and glue it onto your chosen page.

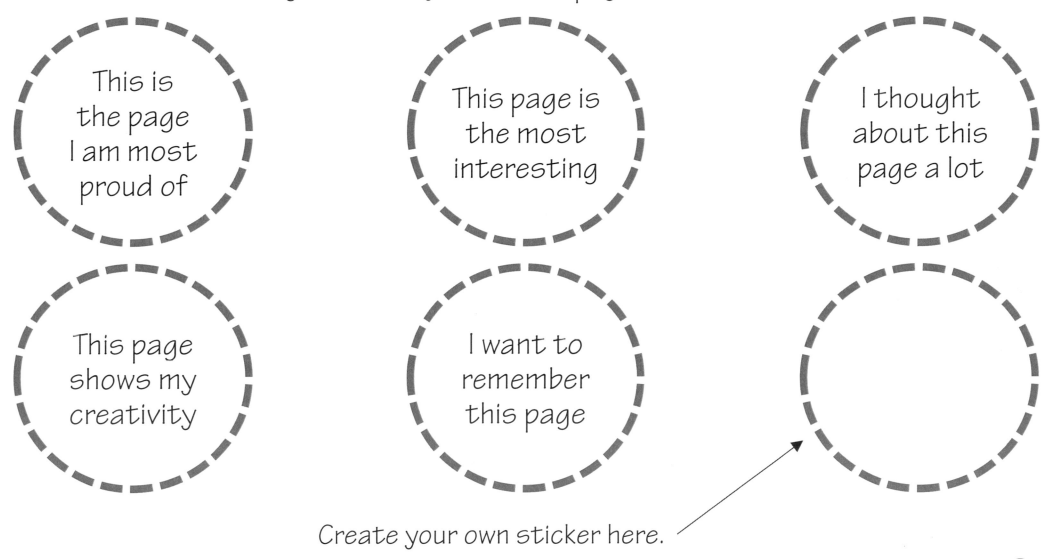

This is the page I am most proud of

This page is the most interesting

I thought about this page a lot

This page shows my creativity

I want to remember this page

Create your own sticker here.

My well-wishes: Ask people to write well-wishes here.

Good luck with your next adventure!